The Illusion of the First Time in Acting

William Gillette, George Arliss

BIBLIOLIFE

PAPERS ON ACTING

I

The Illusion of the First Time in Acting

BY

WILLIAM GILLETTE

WITH AN INTRODUCTION BY

GEORGE ARLISS

Printed for the

Dramatic Museum of Columbia University

in the City of New York

MCMXV

CONTENTS

Introduction by George Arliss 1

The Illusion of the First Time in Acting
    by William Gillette 21

Notes by B. M. 51

THE art of acting is so intimately connected with what is known as "personality" that it is an exceedingly dangerous experiment to attempt to set down in writing any assertion of what methods should be adopted in the making of a good actor and what should be avoided as a preventive measure against becoming a bad one.

There are actors who know every move on the board, whose technic is beyond reproach, who are endowed with those advantages of voice and appearance generally regarded as being "exactly suited to the stage" and who are yet very bad actors indeed. And there are others who are painfully devoid of any visible fitness for their calling, who defy—or rather fail to observe—almost every known canon of stage-technic and who yet succeed in giving the greatest delight to their audiences. The actor of this type is, as a rule, physically and mentally incapable of adopting the acknowledged methods; he "gets across the footlights" without any real knowledge of "how it's done"—by ways that baffle even the expert; he is carried to success almost entirely by what for the moment I will call his personality; he manufactures his methods from material close at hand and seldom borrows or profits by the experience of others. Such an exponent of the art is generally spoken of by his professional brethren as "a very bad actor, but the people like him."

But is he a bad actor merely because he adopts his own methods and knows nothing about the art of other people? Well, I think perhaps he is. Altho he amuses me, I'm afraid he is a bad actor. But he is not as bad as he would be if that other type, who really knows the rules, took him in hand and tried to make him a good actor. Then he would be atrocious. As a matter of fact, he is an actor who can play only one kind of part. But he plays that better than any good actor living. Therefore the public, for whom the theater is run, gets the advantage. His reign lasts just as long as there are plays which require that type. If his part is a prominent one and he makes a very great success, so much the worse for him. He is then placed in an exalted position from which he is bound to fall when the authors have worn themselves out in their frantic endeavor to hold him there; and he will automatically pass from the public ken, destined merely to bob up now and then in a small part that lends itself to his "personality"—and destined to become a disappointed man for the rest of his life.

This actor would never know such bitter disappointment if we could have the ideal condition of stock and repertory companies; he would then find his proper place—which would possibly be that of a valuable "small part" actor for certain "bits." Under present conditions he goes along, possibly for five or six years in a false position—a bad actor disguised by a mere fluke as a good one. In reality his success is merely an adventure. But he doesn't know that. How should he? He is in the position of Christopher Sly—flattered and deceived. But unlike Sly, he is never again able to realize that he is not really a king dethroned by a fickle and ignorant people; and his life is soured for all time. The mere theatergoers may very naturally argue, that as the theater is run for their amusement, and as they pay for its support, they would much prefer to have the "types" selected for each play. Thus they are quite content to have the bad actor in the one part in which he shines, and to allow him to go into oblivion as soon as possible afterwards. There would be something in this argument if the success of plays generally depended mainly on the proper selection of types. But I am convinced that the success of a season's plays, so far as their success shall be swayed by the acting, depends upon the greatest number of actors and actresses who know their business.

I have used the word "personality" because it is difficult to find another word to express the different degrees of that much discust attribute of the actor who is remembered. The personality of the bad actor I have been considering should have a name of its own; it is in reality more of the nature of a deformity. It is generally quite distinct from the personality that helps an actor along to a distinguisht position which he is then able to hold. And, after all, what is this personality that actors are sometimes asked to stifle and at other times counseled to cultivate? Surely it is the Man Himself as he has grown up in his own particular environment. Whether he gets the something that we like about him from his father, or his mother, or his grandfather, doesn't matter. But he certainly hasn't placed it there himself—and he just as certainly cannot remove it. It is inextricably a part of the individual. It is as the egg which is added to enrich the salad in the making. It is part of him as he speaks and lives and has his being. It is that which has made us notice him on the stage. He didn't put it there in order to be noticed; he didn't even know he had it, till we told him so. If personality were merely a particular movement of the eyelid peculiar to the individual, or if it were only the repetition of some unnecessary gesture, it might with some effort be eliminated. But it is so much more. I do not think it fair to an actor to say that he "fits a part to his personality." In studying a part, should he meet with a scene in which he feels he should strike a certain note that he realizes he is physically incapable of reaching, if he then adopts another method which will bring the scene within his range—this is not pandering to his personality; it is merely using legitimately the tools of his trade. Your voice is part of your personality and so is your nose, and so are your eyes and your mouth; so the way you open your mouth and your eyes, and the way you close them again, and the way your head is put on your shoulders, and the way you move those shoulders to which your head is loosely attached.

Now, how is an actor to set about stifling his personality? It will be at once conceded, at any rate by those of experience in acting, that it is an undoubted mistake to attempt to alter one's voice thruout an entire performance. So personality cannot be stifled that way. The mouth may be covered by a large moustache; but in parting with that mouth you are giving up a very eloquent lieutenant that might be most useful during the action of the play. We can let the nose stand, because it is possible that that assists your personality less than any other feature —altho it has its uses. But what about the eyes, and the head that is on *your* shoulders and nobody else's? If they are to be swathed in disguises, you become a lay figure and not a human being at all. No, you must give it up! The ~~only way~~ for you to stifle your personality is to cease to be a person.

On the other hand, how are you going to foster your personality? I confess that I haven't the remotest idea. You may play nothing but footmen, or nothing but gardeners or nothing but gay husbands in French farces, who can all be played one way—but that isn't fostering your personality, that is merely limiting your sphere of experience. There are a great many people on the stage who have peculiarities; but I do not remember any one having been accused by an audience of possessing personality who had not great sincerity. It is the fact that the actor is feeling and living the life of the man he is impersonating that compels his features and his body to have free play, and so the real flesh and blood man is seen. The individuality of the actor cannot be stifled, if the actor himself is feeling and living his part. It may be charged then that personality is a bar to varied characterization. I think not. Let us suppose that it takes one hundred attributes to make a personality, plus a characterization—now it requires only ten of these

to assimilate the character of an old *roué*—
the other ninety are required to make him
a vital human creature. One of the ten is
used to keep the limbs a trifle stiff, another
to give a slight limp perhaps, No. 3 to infuse a little deadness into the eyes, No. 4
to soften the voice, No. 5 to take care of a
slower delivery, and so on. But out of the
remaining ninety flow all the other springs
of life that belong to the actor and are always playing and being drawn upon and gov-
erned by his imagination. Peculiarities and
mannerisms may sometimes attach themselves to personality, but they must in no
wise be regarded as the whole thing. They
may perhaps be units in the hundred, but
they are not what make an actor attractive to
an audience.

Mr. Gillette's situation is, I believe, unique
in the English-speaking world, inasmuch as
he is not only an author of established repu-
tation but has maintained as an actor a position of great distinction for more years than
I feel at liberty to mention without his special permission. And so I feel that his paper
on the 'Illusion of the First Time,' written
as it is with a thoro knowledge of both ends

of the game, and set forth with that expert pen which has helpt (whatever he may say to the contrary) to give him his position as a dramatist, is a very valuable contribution to the literature of the stage.

The Illusion of the First Time, is without doubt of the utmost importance to the full appreciation of any stage performance. Even the professional equilibrist feels this, when he makes two ineffectual efforts to perform his *chef d'oeuvre*,—and then victoriously accomplishes it with that extraordinary assumption of pride and relief that fills our hearts with gladness—when he could have done it quite easily the first time.

But the illusion is, for the actor, not quite so difficult to maintain as might be supposed. The lay members of society (by lay members, I mean those who ask an actor if he will dine with them at 8 o'clock on Monday night) if they think about it at all, suppose that the actor speaks a given number of words every night—for a thousand nights if necessary, without any further inspiration than that which is allowed him by the author, and that which reaches him in the form of handclapping from the lay members themselves.

Of course, if this were so, the length of the working life of an actor could be figured out mathematically, just as the length of the life of a London 'bus horse used to be worked out in advance in the general offices of the Omnibus Company. I believe the life of the 'bus horse came out at three years. I should not give an actor quite so long. I think he would be taken to a lunatic asylum towards the end of the second year. But the thousand influences which inspire an actor and help to give each performance something of the elements of a First Time, can be fully realized only by the person who has been thru it. It is true, there are actors —small part actors—who can go on night after night and speak the same lines and feel no outside influence at all. But then, they don't feel any inside influence either. They are lunatics to start with, or they would never have remained in a calling for which they have not the least aptitude.

But the mental machinery of the actor is even more delicate than the record of a phonograph. That mental needle which acts upon the record of the author's words is influenced by weather, by sudden sounds, by unusual lights, by pains in the back and head, by dinner, by no dinner, by a letter from home, by feeling too well, by not feeling well enough, by no ink in the place where the ink ought to be, by a fear of forgetting, by a sudden awful realization of being stared at by hundreds of pairs of eyes and of not being able to escape. These are only a few of the thousand influences that are entirely apart from the ever varying influence of the pulse of the audience.

But I am not sure that the lay members understand what I mean. I will try to explain. The actor comes on to the stage to play his same part for the 500th time—to go thru the "grind" once more, as he often put its (but seldom means it). The audience is dull, the play is dull, and the whole thing seems a bore. Suddenly the electrician (who is always doing something mysterious at the back of the stage) drops a hundred lamps with a crash;—it is possibly only two or three, but it sounds like a hundred. The spectators hear it, of course, and commence talking pleasantly to one another about it, and fall speculating as to what is really the cause. The actor instantly becomes mad with rage; and the next instant he realizes the necessity of regaining the attention of the audience at once, or allowing the first act to go to pieces. So he "acts for all he's worth" for the next ten minutes and he gradually feels his audience coming back to him. And they become more and more attentive; and the sensation of having brought them back is so pleasant that the actor becomes interested in them personally and feels a certain friendly relationship between them and himself; and for the rest of that performance he gives them the best he has. And something of this kind happens almost every night. The Illusion of the First Time is assisted materially by the fact that the actor is nearly always fighting against some odds. I am speaking now of the time when the play has settled down to a long run. If he is feeling ill, he is anxious that he should not appear so; and he fights against any possible evidence of his pain, mental or physical. If there is an understudy playing, he makes an effort to cover any defect that may thus arise. If there is no ink when there ought to be ink, this is sufficient to break the monotony and to stimulate him to a certain degree of spontaneity.

Then, of course, there is the audience, the great stimulant. One intensely attentive figure in a dull audience, one distinct but invisible chuckle at a pet line, one spontaneous ejaculation expressive of appreciation, will serve to stimulate for a whole evening. Two sneezes, two coughs from the same scoundrel, will put the devil into you and make you swear to yourself that you will keep him quiet or die in the attempt. Then, of course, there is the great concerted influence of an audience, that inspires the actor and lifts him far above himself. This concerted influence is frequently brought about if some petty incident has served to break the monotony of repetition and has aroused in the actor that delightful sensation of spontaneity. These conditions in themselves are not sufficient to prevent an actor from falling into many evil practices which creep in as a result of long familiarity with the author's lines; but they help very considerably.

Mr. Gillette raises an interesting question when he speaks of the necessity of the stage-lover to adopt an artificial method if he desire to please the dramatic critics. I wonder if the critics are not after all right in their attitude. How many authors *write* a love-scene that is a real love-scene? There must be many,—but for the moment I don't recall one. I will even go so far as to sympathize with and forgive the authors for not doing so. I believe that love-scenes in real life are generally spread over a fairly considerable time. They cover several luncheons, and some dinners, possibly an occasional dance, and a number of unexpected meetings in the morning. As a matter of fact, I doubt whether the majority of people who marry for love have ever had a love-scene which, segregated, would be recognized as such. Of course, the author hasn't time for all this—or rather the audience has not. So the lovers have to say it all in words, and in one afternoon—or perhaps in the middle of dinner, or while some mature person is putting on her cloak in the next room. It therefore becomes an artificial love-scene. Now the result of attempting to play an artificial love-scene in a natural way is fatal; it must be played artificially. It is necessary for the actor of these scenes "to stand behind the lady and breathe the love messages down the back of her neck, so that they can both face to the front at the same time." These messages are generally so long, that if she turned her back all the time, the audience might easily imagine she was fast asleep,—unless she moved her shoulders, in which case, it might have some doubt as to whether she was laughing or crying. And if he turned his back to the audience and let her "have the stage" half the people in the house would hear only half he was saying to her, which might be "natural" for the lovers, but it would be very unnatural for the spectators to be there at all, because the only reason they came and paid their money was because they were led to believe they were going to hear it all.

Of course, one can never be really, truly "natural" on the stage. Acting is a bag of tricks. The thing to learn is how to be unnatural, and just how unnatural to be under given conditions. Many plays appear to be natural to the casual audience, but are in reality perfectly artificial from beginning to end. To play these naturally would be equivalent to an artist sticking real leaves on his painted canvas in order to suggest a natural tree. Half the fun and half the art of the actor is to play such pieces artificially while appearing to play them naturally.

Leading actors are continually being blamed for taking the center of the stage and facing the audience. It is called entirely unnatural. It is. But an actor who gets his living by acting will discover that the leading actor generally has the most to say. As he goes thru the country playing in all sorts and sizes of theaters he may find that his manager will come round to him and say "I have had a number of complaints at the box-office lately that you are rather inaudible in some scenes." If the actor shouts he can ruin any scene. Now, the center of the stage is the spot that can be seen easiest by everybody in the house, and in some theaters it is the only spot that can be seen from certain portions of the house. Therefore, I say, use it as much as possible. It has to be admitted that the words of a play are quite necessary to the proper interpretation of an author's work. It has also to be admitted that, speaking generally, the face expresses more to the square inch, by at least one hundred per cent than any other available adjunct in the actor's equipment. Therefore, I say, face the audience as much as possible.

The thing to learn is how to do these things without being found out.

GEORGE ARLISS.

(April, 1915.)

The Illusion of the First Time in Acting

The Illusion of the First Time in Acting

I AM to talk a brief paper this morning on a phase of what is called Drama, by which is meant a certain well-known variety of stage-performance usually but not necessarily taking place in a theater or some such public building, or even transplanted out into the grass, as it occasionally is in these degenerate days.

If you care at all to know how I feel about having to talk on this subject—which I do not suppose you do—but I'll tell you any way—I am not as highly elated at the prospect as you might imagine. Were I about to deliver a Monograph on Medicine or Valuable Observations on Settlement Work and that sort of thing—or even if I had been so particularly fortunate as to discover the Bacillus of Poetry and could now report progress toward the concoction of a serum that would exterminate the disease without killing the poet—that is, without quite killing him,—I could feel that I was doing some good. But I can't do any good to Drama. Nobody can. Nothing that is said or written or otherwise promulgated on the subject will affect it in the slightest degree. And the reason for this rather discouraging view of the matter is, I am sorry to say, the very simplest in the world as well as the most unassailable, and that is, the Record.

And what is meant by a "Record" is, roughly speaking, a History of Behavior along a certain line—a history of what has been done—of what has taken place, happened, occurred—of what effect has been produced in the particular direction under consideration. We might say that Records are past performances or conditions along a specified line.

And upon these Records or Histories of Behavior, Occurrences, or Conditions, depend all that we know or may ever hope to know; for even Experiment and Research are but endeavors to produce or discover Records that have been hidden from our eyes. To know anything—to have any opinion or estimate or knowledge or wisdom worth having, we must take account of Past

Performances, or be aware of the results of their consideration by others—perhaps more expert than we. Yet, notwithstanding this perfectly elementary fact of existence, there is a group or class of these Records, many of them relating to matters of the utmost interest and importance, the consideration of which would at least keep people from being so shamelessly duped and fooled as they frequently are, to which no one appears to pay the slightest attention.

This class or group of forgotten or ignored Items of Behavior I have ventured, for my own amusement, to call the Dead Records—meaning thereby that they are *dead to us*—dead so far as having the slightest effect upon human judgment or knowledge or wisdom is concerned, buried out of sight by our carelessness and neglect. And in this interesting but unfortunate group, and evidently gone to its last long rest, reposes the Record of the Effect upon Drama of what has been said and written about it by scholars and thinkers and critics. And if this Record could be roused to life—that is, to consideration but for a moment, it would demonstrate beyond the shadow of a doubt that Drama is perfectly immune from the maneuvers of any germ that may lurk in what people who are supposed to be "Intellectual" may say or write or otherwise put forth regarding it.

The unending torrent of variegated criticism, condemnation, advice, contempt,—the floods of space-writing, prophesying, high-brow and low-brow dinner-table and midnight-supper anathematizing that has cascaded down upon Drama for centuries has never failed to roll lightly off, like water from the celebrated back of a duck—not even moistening a feather.

From all of which you will be able to infer without difficulty that it is perfectly hopeless for me to try to do any good to Drama. And I can't do it any harm either. Even that would be something. In fact, nothing at all can be done to it. And as I am cut off in that direction there seems to be nothing left but to try if, by describing a rather extraordinary and harassing phase of the subject involving certain conditions and requirements from a Workshop point of view, it is possible so to irritate or annoy those who sit helpless before me, that I can feel something has been accomplisht, even if not precisely what one might wish.

It must be a splendid thing to be able to begin right—to take hold of and wrestle with one's work in life from a firm and reliable standing-ground, and to obtain a comprehensive view of the various recognized divisions, forms, and limitations of what work, so that one may choose with intelligence the most advantageous direction in which to apply his efforts. The followers of other occupations, arts, and professions appear to have these advantages to a greater or less degree, while we who struggle to bring forth attractive material for the theater are without them altogether; and not only without them, but the jumble and confusion in which we find ourselves is infinitely increased by the inane, contradictory, and ridiculous things that are written and printed on the subject. Even ordinary names which might be supposed to define the common varieties of stage work are in a perfectly hopeless muddle. No one that I have ever met or heard of has appeared to know what Melodrama really is; we know very well that it is *not* Drama-with-Music as the word implies. I have askt people who were supposed to have quite powerful intellects (of course the cheap ones can tell you all about it—just as the silliest and most feeble-minded are those who instantly inform you regarding the vast mysteries of the universe) —I say I have made inquiries regarding Melodrama of really intellectual people, and none of them have appeared to be certain. Then there's plain Drama—without the Melo, a very loose word applied to any sort of performance your fancy dictates. And Comedy—some people tell you it's a funny, amusing, laughable affair, and the Dictionaries bear them out in this; while others insist that it is any sort of a play, serious or otherwise, which is not Tragedy or Farce. And there's Farce, which derives itself from force—to stuff,—because it was originally an affair stuffed full of grotesque antics and absurdities;—yet we who have occasion to appear in Farce at the present day very well know that unless it is not only written but performed with the utmost fidelity to life it is a dead and useless thing. In fact it must not by any chance *be* Farce! And there is the good old word play that covers any and every kind of Theatrical Exhibition and a great many other things besides. Therefore, in what appears—at least to us—to be this hopeless confusion, we in the workshops find it necessary to make a classification of Stage Work for our own use. I am not advising anyone else to make it, but am confessing, and with considerable trepidation—for these things are supposed to be scared from human touch that *we* do it. Merely to hint to a real Student of the Drama that such a liberty has been taken would be like shaking a red bull before a rag. Sacrilege is the name of this crime.

More or less unconsciously, they end without giving any names or definitions (I am doing that for you this morning), we who labor in the shops divide Stage Performances in which people endeavor to represent others than themselves for the amusement and edification of spectators, into two sections:

    1.   Drama.

    2.   Other Things.

That's all. Its so simple that I suppose you'll be annoyed with me for talking about it. Drama—in the dictionary which we make for ourselves,—is that form of Play or Stage Representation which expresses what it has to express in Terms of Human Life. Other Things are those which do not. Without doubt those Other Things may be classified in all sorts of interesting and amusing ways, but that is not our department. What we must do is to extricate Drama from among them;—and not only that, but we must carefully clear off and brush away any shreds or patches of them that may cling to it. We do not do this because we want to, but because we have to.

For us, then, Drama is composed of—or its object is attained by—simulated life episodes and complications, serious, tragic, humorous, as the case may be; by the interplay of simulated human passion and human character.

Other Things aim to edify, interest, amuse, thrill, delight, or whatever else they may aim to do, by the employment of language, of voice, of motion, of behavior, etc., as they would not be employed in the natural course of human existence. These unlifelike things, though they may be and fre-

quently are, strecht upon a framework of
Drama, are not Drama; for that framework
so decorated and encumbered can never be
brought to a semblance or a simulation of
life.

Altho I have stated, in order to shock no
one's sensibilities, that this is our own pri-
vate and personal classification of Stage
Work, I want to whisper to you very con-
fidentially that it doesn't happen to be original with us; for the development and spe-
cialization of this great Life-Class, *Drama*—
or whatever you may please to call it, has
been slowly but surely brought about by that
section of the Public which has long patron-
ized the better class of theaters. It has had
no theories—no philosophy—not even a
realization of what it does, but has very well
known what it *wants*—yet by its average and
united choosing has the character of Stage
Work been changed and shaped and molded,
ever developing and progressing by the sur-
vival of that which was fittest to survive in
the curious world of Human Preference.

Be so good as to understand that I am
not advocating this classification in the
slightest degree, or recommending the use of

any name for it. I am merely calling attention to the fact that this Grand Division of Stage Work is here—with us,—at the present day; and not only here, but as a *class* of work—as a method or medium for the expressing of what we have to express—is in exceedingly good condition. After years and centuries of development, always in the direction of the humanities, it closely approximates a perfect instrument, capable of producing an unlimited range of effects, from the utterly trivial and inconsequent to the absolutely stupendous. These may be poetical with the deep and vital poetry of Life itself, rather than the pleasing arrangement of words, thoughts, and phrases; tragical with the quivering tragedy of humanity—not the mock tragedy of vocal heroics; comical with the absolute comedy of human nature and human character—not the forced antics of clowns or the supernatural witticisms of professional humorists.

The possibilities of the instrument as we have it to-day are infinite. But those who attempt to use it—the writers and makers and constructors of Drama, are, of course, very finite indeed. They must, as always, range from the multitudes of poor workers —of the cheap and shallow-minded,—to the few who are truly admirable. I have an impression that the conditions prevailing in other arts and professions are not entirely dissimilar. Some one has whispered that there are quite a few Paintings in existence which could hardly be said to have the highest character; a considerable quantity of third, fourth, and fifth rate Music—and some of no rate at all; and at least six hundred billion trashy, worthless, or even criminally objectionable, Novels. It would not greatly surprise me if we of the theater—even in these days of splendid decadence—had a shade the best of it. But whether we have or have not, the explanation of whatever decline there may be in Dramatic Work is so perfectly simple that it should put to shame the vast army of writers who make their living by formulating indignant inquiries regarding it. For the highest authority in existence has stated in plain language that the true purpose of the Play is to hold the mirror up to Nature —meaning, of course, human nature; and this being done at the present day a child in a kindergarten could see why the reflections in that mirror are of the cheapest, meanest, most vulgar and revolting description. Imagine for one moment what would appear in a mirror that could truthfully reflect, upon being held up to the average Newspaper of to-day in the United States! But I admit that this is an extreme case.

And now I am going to ask you—(but it is one of those questions that orators use with no expectation of an answer)—I am going to inquire if anyone here or anywhere else goes so far as to imagine for an instant that a Drama—a Comedy—a Farce—a Melodrama—or, in one word, a Play, is the manuscript or printed book which is ordinarily handed about as such? And now I will answer myself—as I knew I should all the time. One probably does so imagine unless he has thought about it. Doubtless you all suppose that when a person hands you a play to read he hands you that Play—to read. And I am here with the unpleasant task before me of trying to dislodge this perfectly innocent impression from your minds. The person does nothing of that description. In a fairly similar case he might say, "Here is the Music," putting into your hands some sheets of paper covered with different kinds of dots and things strung along what appears to be a barbed-wire fence. It is hardly necessary to remind you that that is not the Music. If you are in very bad luck it may be a Song that is passed to you, and as you roll it up and put it in your hand-bag or your inside overcoat-pocket, do you really think that is the *Song* you have stuffed in there? If so, how cruel! But no! You are perfectly well aware that it is not the Song which you have in your hand-bag or music-roll, but merely the Directions for a Song. And that Song cannot, does not, and never will exist until the specific vibrations of the atmosphere indicated by those Directions actually take place, and only during the time in which they *are* taking place.

And quite similarly the Music which we imagined in your possession a moment ago was not Music at all, but merely a few sheets of paper on which were written or printed certain Directions for Music; and it will not be Music until those Directions are properly complied with.

And again quite similarly the Play which you were supposed to be holding in your hand is not a Play at all, but simply the written or printed Directions for bringing one into being; and that Play will exist only when these Directions for it are being followed out—and not then unless the producers are very careful about it.

Incredible as it may seem there are people in existence who imagine that they can *read* a Play. It would not surprise me a great deal to hear that there are some present with us this very morning who are in this pitiable condition. Let me relieve it without delay. The feat is impossible. No one on earth can read a Play. You may read the *Directions* for a Play and from these Directions imagine as best you can what the Play would be like; but you could no more read the *Play* than you could read a Fire or an Automobile Accident or a Base-Ball Game. The Play—if it is Drama—does not even *exist* until it appeals in the form of Simulated Life. Reading a list of the things to be said and done in order to make this appeal is not reading the appeal itself.

And now that all these matters have been amicably adjusted, and you have so quietly and peaceably given up whatever delusion you may have entertained as to being able to read a Play, I would like to have you proceed a step further in the direction indicated and suppose that a Fortunate Dramatic Author has entered into a contract with a Fortunate Producing Manager for the staging of his work. I refer to the Manager as fortunate because we will assume that the Dramatist's Work appears promising; and I use the same expression in regard to the Author, as it is taken for granted that the Manager with whom he has contracted is of the most desirable description—one of the essentials being that he is what is known as a Commercial Manager.

If you wish me to classify Managers for you,—or indeed, whether you wish it or not, —I will cheerfully do so. There are precisely two kinds, Commercial Managers and Crazy Managers. The Commercial Managers have from fifty to one hundred and fifty thousand dollars a year rent to pay for their theaters, and, strange as it may seem, their desire is to have the productions they make draw money enough to pay it, together with other large expenses necessary to the operation of a modern playhouse. If you read what is written you will find unending abuse and insult for these men. The followers of any other calling on the face of the earth may be and are commercial with impunity. Artists, Musicians, Opera Singers, Art Dealers, Publishers, Novelists, Dentists, Professors, Doctors, Lawyers, Newspaper and Magazine Men and all the rest—even Secretaries of State—are madly hunting for money. But *Managers*—Scandalous, Monstrous, and Infamous! And because of a sneaking desire which most of them nourish to produce plays that people will go to see, they are the lowest and most contemptible of all the brutes that live. I am making no reference to the managerial abilities of these men; in that they must vary as do those engaged in any other pursuit, from the multitudinous poor to the very few good. My allusion is solely to this everlasting din about their commercialism; and I pause long enough to propound the inquiry whether other things that proceed from intellects so painfully puerile should receive the slightest attention from sensible people.

Well, then, our Book of Directions is in the hands of one of these Wretches, and, thinking well of it, he is about to assemble the various elements necessary to bring the Drama for which it calls into existence. Being a Commercial Person of the basest description he greatly desires it to attract the paying public, *and for this reason* he must give it every possible advantage. In consultation with the Author, with his Stage-Manager and the heads of his Scenic, Electric, and Property Departments he proceeds to the work of complying with the requirements of the Book.

So far as painted, manufactured and mechanical elements are concerned, there is comparatively little trouble. To keep these things precisely as much in the background as they would appear were a similar episode in actual life under observation—*and no more*—is the most pronounced difficulty. But when it comes to the Human Beings required to assume the Characters which the Directions indicate, and not only to assume them but to breathe into them the Breath of Life

—and not the *Breath* of Life alone but all other elements and details and items of Life so far as they can be simulated, many and serious discouragements arise.

For in these latter days Life-Elements are required. Not long ago they were not. In these latter days the merest slip from true Life-Simulation is the death or crippling of the Character involved, and it has thereafter to be dragged thru the course of the play as a disabled or lifeless thing. Not all plays are sufficiently strong in themselves to carry on this sort of morgue or hospital service for any of their important *rôles*.

The perfectly obvious methods of Character Assassination such as the sing-song or "reading" intonation, the exaggerated and grotesque use of gesture and facial expression, the stilted and unnatural stride and strut, cause little difficulty. These, with many other inherited blessings from the Palmy Days when there was acting that really amounted to something, may easily be recognized and thrown out.

But the closeness to Life which now prevails has made audiences sensitive to thousands of minor things that would not formerly have affected them. To illustrate my meaning, I am going to speak of two classes of these defects. I always seem to have two classes of everything—but in this case it isn't so. There are plenty more where these two came from. I select these two because they are good full ones, bubbling over with Dramatic Death and Destruction. One I shall call—to distinguish it, the 'Neglect of the Illusion of the First Time'; the other, the 'Disillusion of Doing it Correctly.' There is an interesting lot of them which might be assembled under the heading the 'Illusion of Unconsciousness of What Could Not Be Known'—but there will not be time to talk about it. All these groups, however, are closely related, and the First Time one is fairly representative. And of course I need not tell you that we have no names for these things—no groups—no classification; we merely fight them as a whole—as an army or mob of enemies that strives for the downfall of our Life-Simulation, with poisoned javelins. I have separated a couple of these poisons so that you may see how they work, and incidentally how great little things now are.

Unfortunately for an actor (to save time I mean all known sexes by that), unfortunately for an actor he knows or is supposed to know his part. He is fully aware—especially after several performances—of what he is going to say. The Character he is representing, however, does *not* know what he is going to say, but, if he is a human being, various thoughts occur to him one by one, and he puts such of those thoughts as he decides to, into such speech as he happens to be able to command at the time. Now it is a very difficult thing—and even now rather an uncommon thing—for an actor who knows exactly what he is going to say to behave exactly as tho he didn't; to let his thought (apparently) occur to him as he goes along, even tho they are there in his mind already; and (apparently) to search for and find the words by which to express those thoughts, even tho these words are at his tongue's very end. That's the terrible thing—at his tongue's very end! Living and breathing creatures do not carry their words in that part of their systems; they have to find them and send them there—with more or less rapidity according to their facility in that respect—as occasion arises. And audiences of today, without knowing the nature of the fatal malady are fully conscious of the untimely demise of the Character when the actor portraying it apparently fails to do this.

In matters of speech, of pauses, of giving a Character who would think time to think; in behavior of eyes, nose, mouth, teeth, ears, hands, feet, etc., while he does think and while he selects his words to express the thought—this ramifies into a thousand things to be considered in relation to the language or dialog alone.

This menace of Death from Neglect of the Illusion of the First Time is not confined to matters and methods of speech and mentality, but extends to every part of the presentation, from the most climacteric and important action or emotion to the most insignificant item of behavior—a glance of the eye at some unexpected occurrence—the careless picking up of some small object which (supposedly) has not been seen or handled before. Take the simple matter of entering a room to which, according to the plot or story, the Character coming in is supposed to be a stranger; unless there is vigilance the actor will waft himself blithely across the threshold, conveying the impression that he has at least been born in the house—finding it quite unnecessary to look where he is going and not in the least worth while to watch out for thoughtless pieces of furniture that may, in their ignorance of his approach, have established themselves in his path. And the different scenes with the different people; and the behavior resulting from *their* behavior; and the love-scenes as they are called— these have a little tragedy all their own for the performers involved; for, if an actor plays his part in one of these with the gentle awkwardness and natural embarrassment of one in love for the first time—as the plot supposes him to be—he will have the delight of reading the most withering and caustic ridicule of himself in the next day's papers, indicating in no polite terms that he is an awkward amateur who does not know his business, and that the country will be greatly relieved if he can see his way clear to quitting the stage at once; whereas if he behaves with the careless ease and grace and fluency of the Palmy Day Actor, softly breathing airy and poetic love-messages down the back of the lady's neck as he feelingly stands behind her so that they can both face to the front at the same time, the audience will be perfectly certain that the young man has had at least fifty-seven varieties of love-affairs before and that the plot has been shamelessly lying about him.

The foregoing are a few only of the numberless parts or items in Drama-Presentation which must conform to the Illusion of the First Time. But this is one of the rather unusual cases in which the sum of all the parts does *not* equal the whole. For altho every single item from the most important to the least important be successfully safeguarded, there yet remains the Spirit of the Presentation as a whole. Each successive audience before which it is given must feel —not think or reason about, but *feel*—that it is witnessing, not one of a thousand weary repetitions, but a Life Episode that is being lived just across the magic barrier of the footlights. That is to say, the Whole must have that indescribable Life-Spirit or Effect which produces the Illusion of Happening for the First Time. Worth his weight in something extremely valuable is the Stage-Director who can conjure up this rare and precious spirit!

The dangers to dramatic life and limb from the 'Disillusion of Doing it Correctly' are scarcely less than those in the First Time class, but not so difficult to detect and eliminate. Speaking, breathing, walking, sitting, rising, standing, gesturing—in short behaving correctly, when the character under representation would not naturally or customarily do so, will either kill that character outright or make it very sick indeed. Drama can make its appeal only in the form of Simulated Life as it is Lived—not as various authorities on Grammar, Pronunciation, Etiquet, and Elocution happen to announce at that particular time that it ought to be lived.

But we find it well to go much further than the keeping of studied and unusual correctness *out*, and to put common and to-be-expected errors *in*, when they may be employed appropriately and unobtrusively. To use every possible means and device for giving Drama that which makes it Drama—Life-Simulation—must be the aim of the modern Play-Constructor and Producer. And not alone ordinary errors but numberless individual habits, traits, peculiarities are of the utmost value for this purpose.

Among these elements of Life and Vitality but greatly surpassing all others in importance is the human characteristic or essential quality which passes under the execrated name of Personality. The very word must send an unpleasant shudder through this highly sensitive assembly; for it is supposed to be quite the proper and highly cultured thing to sneer at Personality as an altogether cheap affair and not worthy to be associated for a moment with what is highest in Dramatic Art. Nevertheless, cheap or otherwise, inartistic or otherwise, and whatever it really is or is not, it is the most singularly important factor for infusing the Life-Illusion into modern stage creations that is known to man. Indeed, it is something a great deal more than important, for in these days of Drama's close approximation to Life, it is essential. As no human being exists without Personality of one sort or another, an actor who omits it in his impersonation of a human being omits one of the vital elements of existence.

In all the history of the stage no performer has yet been table to simulate or make us of a Personality not his own. Individual tricks, mannerisms, peculiarities of speech and action may be easily accomplisht. They are the capital and stock in trade of the Character Comedian and the Lightning Change Artist, and have nothing whatever to do with Personality.

The actors of recent times who have been universally acknowledged to be great have invariably been so because of their successful use of their own strong and compelling Personalities in the *rôles* which they made famous. And when they undertook parts, as they occasionally did, unsuited to their Personalities, they were great no longer and frequently quite the reverse. The elder Salvini's Othello towered so far above all other renditions of the character known to modern times that they were lost to sight below it. His Gladiator was superb. His Hamlet was an unfortunate occurrence. His personality was marvelous for Othello and the Gladiator, but unsuited to the Dane. Mr. Booth's

personality brought him almost adoration in
his Hamlet—selections from it served him
well in Iago, Richelieu, and one or two other
rôles, but for Othello it was not all that
could be desired. And Henry Irving and
Ellen Terry and Modjeska, Janauschek and
Joseph Jefferson and Mary Anderson, each
and every one of them with marvelous skill
transferred their Personalities to the appro-
priate *rôles.* Even now—once in a while—
one may see Rip Van Winkle excellently well
played, but without Mr. Jefferson's Personality. There it is in simple arithmetic for
you—a case of mere subtraction.

As indicated a moment ago I am only too
well aware that the foregoing view of the
matter is sadly at variance with what we are
told is the Highest Form of the Actor's Art.
According to the deep thinkers and writers
on matters of the theater, the really great
actor is not one who represents with marvelous power and truth to life the characters
within the limited scope of his Personality,
but the performer who is able to assume an
unlimited number of totally divergent *rôles.*
It is not the thing at all to consider a single
magnificent performance such as Salvini's

Othello, but to discover the Highest Art we must inquire how many kinds of things the man can do. This, you will observe, brings it down to a question of pure stage gymnastics. Watch the actor who can balance the largest number of *rôles* in the air without allowing any of them to spill over. Doubtless an interesting exhibition if you are looking for that form of sport. In another art it would be: "Do not consider this man's paintings, even tho masterpieces, for he is only a Landscape Artist. Find the chap who can paint forty different kinds." I have an idea the Theater-going Public is to be congratulated that none of the great Stage Performers, at any rate of modern times, has entered for any such competition.

NOTES

NOTES

THIS address was delivered at the fifth joint-session of the American Academy of Arts and Letters and of the National Institute of Arts and Letters, held in Chicago on November 14, 1913; and it was afterward written out for publication in the seventh number of the proceedings of the Academy and Institute (pp. 16-24).

In this paper there are four points made with special emphasis as tho to challenge contradition. These may be summarily described as the assertions

(A) that a play has to be seen to yield up its dramatic value;

(B) that the manager of a theater must be commercial or crazy;

(C) that the actor must convey the illusion that what he is doing is then done for the first time;

(D) and that an actor is most successful when he can infuse his part with his own personality.

Any reader inclined to pick up the glove of the challenger and to impale himself upon one or another of these points will do well to remember that they are each of them supported by authorities not lightly to be impeacht.

(A). Goethe in his 'Conversations with Eckermann' dwelt more than once on the difficulty, not to say the impossibility, of judging a play from a mere perusal of the manuscript and of estimating the effect which might be produced by an actual performance. Molière, in the preface to the 'Précieuses Ridicules,' explained his original intention not to publish that play as due to his knowledge that a large portion of the beauties which had been found in it depended on the gestures and on the voices of the performers, and that therefore he felt disinclined to print his play in a book wherein it would be deprived of these necessary ornaments. The younger Dumas, in the preface to the 'Père Prodigue' declared dramatic effect to be sometimes so intangible that the spectator cannot find it in the printed text the point which delighted him in the performance of a play and which was due perhaps to "a word, a look, a gesture, a silence, a purely atmospheric condition."

Altho any one holding in his hand the words and music of a song does not actually possess that song until it is really sung by a human voice in accord with those directions, yet there are experts whom insight and experience enable to make a better guess at the probable effect of the unsung song than would be possible to the average lover of music devoid of this equipment; and in like manner there are a few readers of plays, possessing a similar insight and experience which enable them to make a better guess at the effect of the unperformed drama than is possible to the average reader less substantially trained and less gifted with interpretative imagination. Fleeming Jenkin, so Robert Louis Stevenson recorded in his memoir of his friend, was "one of the not very numerous people who can read a play: a knack, the fruit of much knowledge and some imagination, comparable to that of reading score."

(B). In support of this second point, that the manager of a theater is unwise unless he pays respect to the economic stability of his enterprise, it is possible to cite another of Goethe's remarks to Eckermann. He asserted (May 1, 1825) that Shakspere and Molière had always a keen eye to the main chance and that "both of them wisht, above all things, to make money by their theaters. . . . Nothing is more dangerous for the well-being of a theater than when the director is so placed, that a greater or less receipt at the treasury does not affect him personally. . . . It is a property of human nature soon to relax when not impelled by personal advantage or disadvantage." It is perhaps not unfair to suggest that Goethe may have moved to this declaration by his own experience as manager of the ducal theater at Weimar, and by his memory of the unsatisfactory results of his occasional refusals to give due weight to the wishes of the playgoers who paid their way in. With these quotations from his table-talk may be compared the more deliberate presentation of the case in the prolog to 'Faust' in which the manager is allowed to state his views at length.

(C). In Francis Wilson's 'Joseph Jefferson: Reminiscences of a Fellow-Player' there are several passages which bear upon the necessity for creating the Illusion of the First Time. "The actor," said the great comedian, "must not only produce, but in order to make the greatest artistic effect, he must reproduce each time as if he had never produced before," (p. 100). And again, in addressing the students of the American Academy of Dramatic Arts in April, 1897, Jefferson told these apprentice players, that their profession was "not only one of production but also of reproduction. A writer does not write the same book, a painter does not paint the same picture; but you have to play the same part very often,—night after night—and yet play as if you never had played it before," (p. 109).

On one occasion a ten year old boy who had seen 'Rip Van Winkle' was introduced to Jefferson and informed that he was talking to the performer of the part. The boy lookt up at the actor and said in the most childish and frank manner, "Don't you remember that time when your gun fell apart?" And Jefferson joyfully commented: "*That* time, and it had fallen apart for *thousands* of times!" And he told the boy's father that the little lad had paid him the best compliment he had ever had in his life,—for "if I made him believe that was the first time that gun had fallen apart, I did much better than I thought I did," (p. 138).

An even more striking illustration of the necessity of creating the Illusion of the First Time is to be found in Jefferson's own 'Autobiography' (pp. 443-4) where he reports a conversation between Macready and Mrs. Warner:—"My dear Madam," said Macready, "you have acted with me in the tragedy of 'Werner' for many years. . . . I have noticed lately that some passages do not produce the effect they formerly did. There is a certain speech especially that seems to have lost its power. . . . the one wherein Werner excuses himself to his son for the 'petty plunder' of Stralenheim's gold.

In our earlier performances . . . this apology was received with markt favor; and last evening it produced no apparent effect. Can you form any idea why this should be? Is it that the audience has grown too familiar with the story? I must beg you to be candid with me."

And Mrs. Warner answered, "since you desire that I should speak plainly, I do not think it is because your audience is too familiar with the story, but because you are too familiar with it yourself. . . . When you spoke that speech ten years ago there was a surprise in your face as tho you only then realized what you had done. You looked shockt and bewildered, and in a forlorn way seemed to cast about for words that would excuse the crime; and all this with a depth of feeling and sincerity that would naturally come from an honest man who had been for the first time in his life accused of theft. [But now] you speak it like one who has committed a great many thefts in his life and whose glib excuses are so pat and frequent that he is neither shockt, surprized or abasht at the accusation."

Jefferson heard this anecdote from C. W. Couldock and he recognized its force at once:—"I knew then that I had been unconsciously falling into the same error, and I felt that the fault would increase rather than diminish with the time, if I could not hit upon some method to check it. I began by listening to each important question as tho it had been given for the first time, turning the query over in my mind and then discussing it, even at times hesitating as if for want of words to frame the reply."

Henry Irving, in an address on the 'Art of Acting,' delivered at Harvard University in 1885, is in accord with Jefferson: "It is necessary that the actor should learn to think before he speaks: a practise which, I believe, is very useful off the stage. Let him remember . . . that the thought precedes the word. . . . Often it will be found that the most natural, the most seemingly accidental effects are obtained when the working of the mind is seen before the tongue gives it words."

(D). Here again a quotation may be adduced from Wilson's 'Jefferson': "It is a great mistake for the artist to attempt entirely to sink his individuality in the parts he assumes. By so doing he is robbing the audience of that for which they are looking, that for which they admire him," (pp. 221-2). And Ellen Terry, in her appreciation of the 'Russian Ballet' takes occasion to remark that it used to be said of Henry Irving, "who exprest himself in a multiplicity of parts, that he was always the same Irving.

Certainly he was always faithful to himself, whatever he assumed. This is a sign of the presence of genius, not of its absence," (p. 17).

It may be well also to call attention to the fact that nearly all of the great actors have been men of markt individuality and that they have rarely sought to disguise their personalities in their several performances. When they were impersonating any one of the chief characters of the drama they brought into vigorous relief those characteristics which were in accord with their own temperament and therefore within their means of expression. A great actor does not necessarily play a great part as he thinks that it ought to be played but rather as he feels that he himself can best play it. Fanny Kemble, it is significant to record, held that her aunt, Mrs. Siddons, "could lay no claim to versatility—it was not in her nature; she was without mobility of mind, countenance or manner; and her dramatic organization was in that respect inferior to Garrick's; but out of a family of twenty-eight persons, all of whom made the stage their vocation, she alone preëminently combined the qualities requisite to make a great theatrical performer in the highest degree."

B. M.

CPSIA information can be obtained at www.ICGtesting.com
Printed in the USA
LVOW12s1928100813

347242LV00003B/91/A

9 781103 778324